MAMMALS

PREDATORS

Written by
Mignonne Gunasekara

BookLife
PUBLISHING

©2020
BookLife Publishing Ltd.
King's Lynn
Norfolk PE30 4LS

ISBN: 978-1-83927-257-8

Written by:
Mignonne Gunasekara

Edited by:
Shalini Vallepur

Designed by:
Amy Li

A catalogue record for this book is available from the British Library.

CONTENTS

Words that look like this can be found in the glossary on page 24.

MEET THE PREDATORS

Welcome to the world of predators. Predators are animals that hunt other animals for food. They come in many shapes and sizes, but they all have something in common – to their <u>prey</u>, they are terrifying!

Mammals are warm-blooded animals that feed their babies on milk they make themselves.

In this book, we will be looking at predators that are mammals. They can look cute when they are babies... but they grow up to be strong and deadly hunters.

AFRICAN WILD DOG

African wild dogs are also known as painted dogs. They are <u>endangered</u> because of people. They live and hunt in groups called packs, and can run at more than 70 kilometres per hour.

Big ears

Sharp teeth

Every dog has a pattern of fur that is special to them.

African wild dogs usually hunt antelopes, such as gazelles. Packs can work together to hunt animals as big as wildebeests.

Fact File

Habitat: <u>Desert</u>, forest, <u>grassland</u>

Weapons: Speed, teeth

Prey: Antelopes, wildebeests, warthogs, rats, birds

7

HONEY BADGER

Honey badgers are also known as ratels. They are called honey badgers because they break into beehives to eat honey and bee <u>larvae</u>.

Long, sharp claws

Honey badgers use their long claws to dig and break open beehives.

Honey badgers have very thick skin. This protects them from the stings and bites of _venomous_ prey, such as scorpions and snakes.

Honey badgers are not hurt when they eat venomous prey.

Fact File

Habitat: Mountain, desert, grassland, _rainforest_

Weapons: Strong teeth, long claws

Prey: Insects, reptiles, birds, small mammals

9

LION

Lions are big cats that live in a family group called a pride. An adult male lion usually has long hair growing around its head. This is called a mane.

Mane

Male lion

Female lion

Female lions often do most of the hunting for the pride.

Lions usually hunt at night. They can work together to hunt animals that are bigger than themselves. Lions also steal food from other predators.

Fact File

Habitat: Grassland, open woodland

Weapons: Sharp teeth, claws

Prey: Zebras, wildebeests, antelopes

Sharp teeth

POLAR BEAR

Sharp teeth

Polar bears have large front paws that help them swim. They are the largest <u>carnivores</u> to live on land and their main prey is seals.

Strong claws

Polar bears have black skin underneath their fur.

12

Polar bears use their sharp, strong claws to catch and kill prey.

Polar bears hunt by waiting near gaps in the ice for a seal to pop up. They also eat dead animals they find, such as whales.

Fact File

Habitat: Sea ice of the Arctic Ocean

Weapons: Strong, sharp claws

Prey: Seals, fish

FISHING CAT

Fishing cats are found in South and Southeast Asia. They live in <u>wetland</u> habitats but also hunt near farms and towns.

Sharp teeth

Fishing cats mostly eat fish.

Fishing cats are good swimmers. They have two layers of fur in their coats. This stops water from reaching their skin as they swim.

Fishing cats will happily get in the water to hunt fish.

Fact File

Habitat: Wetland, near towns

Weapons: Claws, teeth

Prey: Fish, birds, frogs

ORCA

Orcas are also known as killer whales. They live in family groups called pods. Orcas are very clever animals. Pods can work together to take down prey bigger than themselves, such as whales.

Powerful tail

An orca's teeth can grow to be ten centimetres long.

An orca can make sounds that travel underwater until they hit an object. The sounds then bounce back to the orca. This tells the orca where the object is. This is called echolocation.

Orcas use echolocation to talk to each other and hunt prey such as penguins.

Fact File

Habitat: Every ocean in the world

Weapons: Cleverness, powerful tail, teeth, speed

Prey: Fish, seals, seabirds, squid, whales

17

GREY WOLF

Grey wolves live in family groups called packs. They can travel large distances in a day. Grey wolves can run at speeds of around 60 kilometres per hour.

Sharp teeth for tearing meat

Wolves can go without food for a few days. When they do find food, they can eat a lot of it at once. This keeps them going until they can find more food.

Wolves in a pack can work together to hunt prey that are bigger than themselves.

Fact File

Habitat: Forest, desert

Weapons: Speed, sense of smell, sharp teeth

Prey: Deer, elk, moose, bison, fish

19

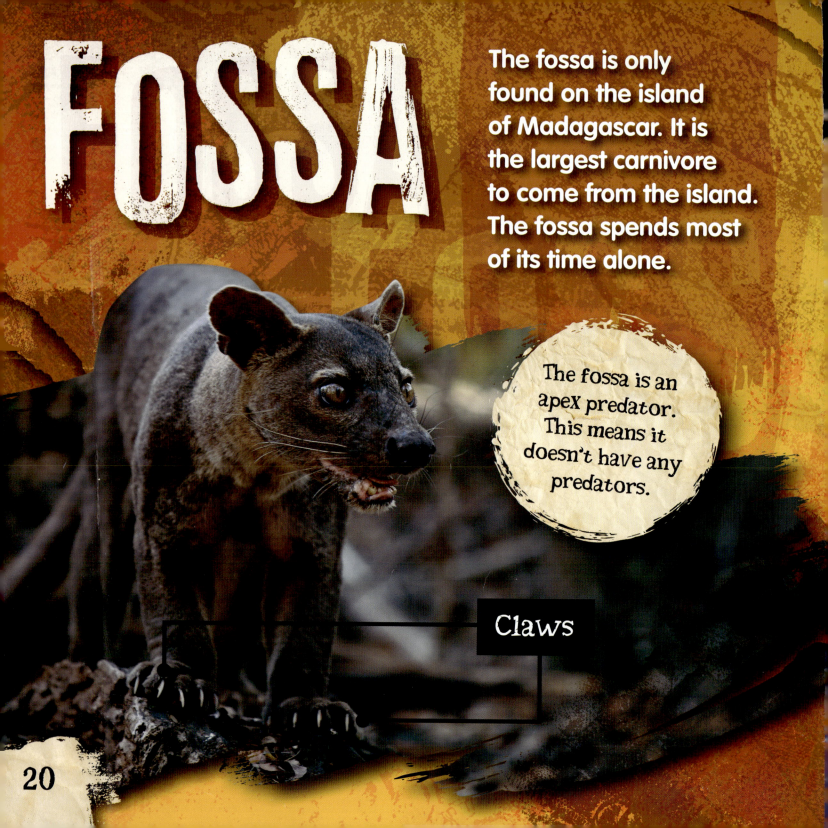

FOSSA

The fossa is only found on the island of Madagascar. It is the largest carnivore to come from the island. The fossa spends most of its time alone.

The fossa is an apex predator. This means it doesn't have any predators.

Claws

Lemurs are the fossa's main prey. The fossa has a long tail that helps it balance as it moves through the trees.

The fossa has a tail that is about as long as its body!

Sharp teeth

Fact File

Habitat: Forest

Weapons: Sharp teeth, sharp claws

Prey: Lemurs, mice, wild pigs, birds, fish

ON YOUR MARKS

Congratulations, you met the predators! Weren't they fierce? Some of them are pretty quick too. Let's see how fast they can run in a race.

Orca

60 kilometres per hour

Grey wolf

Around 55 kilometres per hour

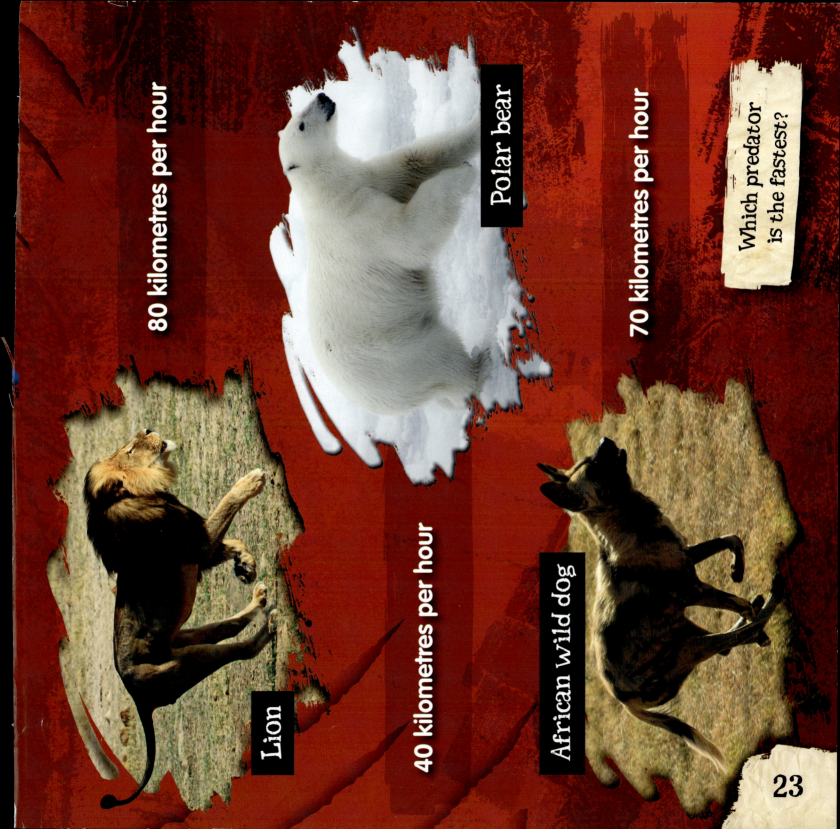

80 kilometres per hour

Polar bear

Which predator
is the fastest?

70 kilometres per hour

Lion

40 kilometres per hour

African wild dog

23

GLOSSARY

carnivores   animals that eat other animals, instead of plants

desert   a place that gets very little rain and where very few plants and animals can live

endangered   when a species of animal is in danger of no longer existing

grassland   an area of land where grass is the main plant that grows there

habitat   the natural home in which animals, plants and other living things live

larvae   young insects that must grow and change before they become adults

prey   animals that are hunted by other animals for food

rainforest   a forest that gets a lot of rainfall

venomous   able to poison another animal through a bite or a scratch

wetland   an area of land that is very wet or covered in water

INDEX

Photo Credits. All images courtesy of Shutterstock. With thanks to Getty Images, Thinkstock Photo and iStockphoto.

Recurring images – Ameena Matcha (old paper), teacept (header font), Alexey Pushkin (grunge texture), MrNoe (claw marks), Olga_C, Ografica (grunge shapes). Cover – Quick Shot, The Len, p2–3 – The Len, p4–5 – Stu Porter, Wildlife World, p6–7 – Ondrej Prosicky, Ewan Chesser, p8–9 – Erwin Niemand, Vladimir Wrange, p10–11 – Maggy Meyer, DDniki, rafaellsilveira, p12–13 – Ondrej Prosicky, Zhiltsov Alexandr, p14–15 – PhotocechCZ, PACO COMO, Vladimir Wrangel, p16–17 – Stephen Lew, Tory Kallman, p18–19 – Thyrymn2, Holly Kuchera, Geoffrey Kuchera, p20–21 – Dmitry Shkurin, Dudarev Mikhail, Miroslav Halama, p22–23 – Anette Holmberg, Herbert Kratky, paula frenc, Warren Metcalf, wildestanimal